SiNGiNG
iN THE RAiN

for everyone who smiles in the rain!

A big thank you to my editor Peter Marley and art director Jo Cameron for their inspiration and enthusiasm.

First published in 2017 by Oxford University Press

ISBN 978-1-338-29829-1

12 11 10 9 8 7 6 5 4 3 18 19 20 21 22 23

Printed in the U.S.A. 40

First Scholastic printing, March 2018

The drawings in this book were created using watercolors, pencil, and calligraphy ink, then collaged and colored using QuarkXpress and Adobe Photoshop.

SINGING IN THE RAIN

BASED ON THE SONG BY
ARTHUR FREED AND NACIO HERB BROWN

PICTURES BY
tim hopgood

SCHOLASTIC INC.

I'm **singing** in the rain,
just singing in the rain.

What a **glorious** feeling . . .

I'm **happy** again.

I'm laughing at clouds, so dark up above.

The sun's in my heart and I'm ready for love.

Let the stormy clouds **chase**

everyone from the **place.**

Come on with the rain . . .

I've a **smile** on my face.

I walk down the lane, with a **happy** refrain.

And
I'm
singing,

just
singing

in the rain.

I'm **singing** in the rain,

just singing in the rain.

What a **glorious** feeling . . .

I'm
happy
again.

I'm laughing at clouds,
so dark up above.

The sun's in my heart

and I'm ready for love.

Let the stormy clouds **chase**

everyone from the **place**.

Come on with the rain . . .

I've a **smile** on my face.

I walk
down
the lane,
with a
happy
refrain.

And I'm singing . . .

. . . just singing in the rain!

SINGING IN THE RAIN

BASED ON THE SONG BY
ARTHUR FREED AND NACIO HERB BROWN

I'm singing in the rain,
just singing in the rain.
What a glorious feeling,
I'm happy again.

I'm laughing at clouds,
so dark up above.
The sun's in my heart
and I'm ready for love.

Let the stormy clouds chase,
everyone from the place.
Come on with the rain,
I've a smile on my face.

I walk down the lane,
with a happy refrain.
And I'm singing,
just singing in the rain.

Apart from "**SINGING IN THE RAIN**" being the centerpiece to one of my favorite films, the reason I chose to illustrate this song is its underlying positive message. As adults, it is easy to forget the joy of rain.

We tend to view it as an inconvenience rather than the wonderful thing that it is. Rain is something beautiful that connects all life, from the city to the rain forest. So next time it rains, don't stay indoors. Go outside and soak it up like the children in this book. What a glorious feeling it is!

timhopgood